EXPLANATORY NOTES

Prevention of Terrorism Act 2005

Chapter 2

£5.00

PREVENTION OF TERRORISM ACT 2005

EXPLANATORY NOTES

INTRODUCTION

1.   These explanatory notes relate to the Prevention of Terrorism Act 2005 which received Royal Assent on 11 March 2005. They have been prepared by the Home Office in order to assist the reader in understanding the Act. They do not form part of the Act and have not been endorsed by Parliament.

2.   The notes need to be read in conjunction with the Act. They are not, and are not meant to be, a comprehensive description of the Act. So where a section or part of a section does not seem to require an explanation or comment, none is given.

SUMMARY

3.   The purpose of this Act is to provide for the making of 'control orders' imposing obligations on individuals suspected of being involved in terrorism-related activity. These are preventative orders which are designed to restrict or prevent the further involvement by individuals in such activity.

4.   A control order may impose any obligations necessary for purposes connected with preventing or restricting an individual's further involvement in terrorism-related activity. The intention is that each order will be tailored to the particular risk posed by the individual concerned. Obligations that may be imposed include, for example, prohibitions on the possession or use of certain items, restrictions on movement to or within certain areas, restrictions on communications and associations, and requirements as to place of abode. It will be possible to make control orders against any individuals suspected of involvement in terrorism-related activity, irrespective of nationality, or terrorist cause.

5.   Control orders that do not involve derogating from the European Convention on Human Rights (ECHR), called 'non-derogating control orders', will be made by the Secretary of State. The Secretary of State must seek permission from the court to make a non-derogating control order. However, in cases of urgency, the Secretary of State can make an order without first seeking the permission of the court but he must refer it immediately to the court for confirmation. Control orders that do involve derogating from the ECHR will be made by the court itself on application from the Secretary of State. Such control orders are called 'derogating control orders'. All

control orders will be subject to full hearings by the High Court or Court of Session. There will be a right of appeal on a point of law from a decision of the High Court or Court of Session.

6.   Breach of an obligation imposed by a control order, without reasonable excuse, will be a criminal offence punishable, following conviction on indictment, with a prison sentence of up to 5 years, or a fine, or both; or, following summary conviction, to a prison sentence of up to 12 months (or 6 months in Scotland or Northern Ireland), or a fine, or both.

7.   Features of the new scheme will include:

- Supervision by the court of the making of non-derogating control orders;

- Power of the court to make derogating control orders on application from the Secretary of State;

- Control order proceedings involving the hearing of evidence in open and closed session with Special Advocates representing the interests of the individuals concerned in the latter;

- The application of a judicial review test in hearings relating to non-derogating control orders;

- the application of the civil standard of proof on the question of involvement in terrorism-related activity in hearings relating to derogating control orders;

- Independent review of the operation of the Act with the first review to be carried out after the Act has been in operation for nine months and subsequent reviews to be carried out annually;

- Reports by the Secretary of State to Parliament every three months on his exercise of the control order powers during that period;

- Where a derogation is in place which has been approved by Parliament, the need for further annual Parliamentary approval of the continuing need to rely on the derogation to make derogating control orders.

OVERVIEW

8.   The Act is arranged as follows:

Control orders

9.　　Sections 1 – 9 relate to the circumstances in which control orders may be made, their duration and the obligations (including penalties) attached to them.

10.　　This part of the Act describes the tests which the Secretary of State or court must apply in determining whether a control order may be made against an individual, and the obligations which may be imposed by the order. The Act provides an illustrative list of the obligations to which an individual may be subject and specifies penalties for failing, without reasonable excuse, to observe any obligations so imposed and for intentionally obstructing a person delivering a notice setting out the terms of the order.

11.　　The Act provides that the Secretary of State must obtain permission from the court before making a non-derogating control order. However, if a non-derogating control order has to be imposed urgently, the Secretary of State can make the order straight away but must refer it to the court immediately for the court to consider whether to confirm it. When considering whether to grant permission for a non-derogating control order to be made, and when considering whether to confirm a non-derogating control order that was made urgently, the court may hold an ex parte hearing and must consider whether the Secretary of State's decision in each case was obviously flawed. If it finds that it was, the order cannot be made or must be quashed; if it finds that it was not, the court must refer the control order to a full inter partes hearing which will apply a judicial review test to the control order in order to decide if it, and the obligations it imposes, should continue in force.

12.　　At a full hearing of a non-derogating order, the Court must consider whether any of the following decisions of the Secretary of State were flawed:

- his decision that there are reasonable grounds for suspecting that the person was involved in terrorism-related activity;

- his decision that a control order is necessary for purposes connected with protecting members of the public from the risk of terrorism; and

- his decisions on the imposition of each of the obligations imposed by the order.

13.　　The Act provides that the Secretary of State will apply to the court to make a derogating control order. At a preliminary hearing (which may be ex parte), the court will decide if there is a prima facie case for the order to be imposed. If it finds that there is not, it will not make the order; if it finds that there is, it will make the order and give directions for a full inter partes hearing to be held.

14.   The court will confirm a derogating control order at a full hearing if:

- it is satisfied, on the balance of probabilities, that the controlled person is or has been involved in terrorism-related activity;

- it considers that the obligations imposed as part of the control order are necessary for purposes connected with protecting members of the public from a risk of terrorism;

- it appears to the court that the risk arises out of or is associated with a public emergency in respect of which there is a designated derogation from the whole or a part of Article 5 of the ECHR; and

- the obligations imposed by the control order are in a list of derogating obligations set out in the designation order.

15.   In full hearings on control orders, the court can quash the control order, modify the obligations which it imposes or, in the case of non-derogating control orders, give directions to the Secretary of State to revoke or modify the control order.

16.   The Secretary of State or court (in the case of non-derogating and derogating control orders respectively) may revoke or modify an order at any time.

17.   The Act lists the offences associated with breaching an order or obstructing those exercising statutory powers in relation to an order and the relevant penalties.

Appeals and other proceedings

18.   Sections 10-12 deal with appeals and other proceedings. A person subject to a non-derogating control order may appeal to the court against the following decisions of the Secretary of State:

- his decision to renew the control order;

- his decision to modify the control order;

- his decision not to revoke or modify the control order on an application from the controlled person.

19.   These provisions set out the powers of the court on such appeals.

20.   They also deal with the jurisdiction of the court in relation to control order decisions and derogation matters and the effect of the court's decisions on earlier

convictions.

Supplemental

21.   This part of the Act makes provision for the general oversight of the operation of the Act including independent annual review and three monthly reporting to Parliament on the exercise of his control order powers by the Secretary of State and annual renewal of the provisions.

22.   It also contains general provisions concerning interpretation, repeals, commencement, the title of the Act and extent.

COMMENTARY

Section 1: Power to make control orders

Subsections (1) to (3)

23.   Subsection (1) defines control orders. Subsection (2) explains that control orders may be made by the Secretary of State unless they involve obligations that are incompatible with Article 5 of the ECHR. If they involve such obligations, they can be made only by the court on an application by the Secretary of State. Subsection (3) states that the obligations that may be imposed as part of a control order must be those considered necessary for purposes connected with preventing or restricting involvement by the controlled person in terrorism-related activity.

Subsections (4) to (8)

24.   Subsection (4) sets out an illustrative list of obligations that may be imposed as part of a control order. Subsection (5) confirms that a control order may restrict a person's movements by, for example, requiring him to stay in a particular place at particular times or generally. Subsection (6) explains that controlled persons may be required to cooperate with practical arrangements for monitoring control orders, such as wearing and maintaining apparatus as directed. Subsection (7) provides that information that the controlled person may be required to provide under a control order includes advance information about his proposed movements or other activities. Subsection (8) provides that a particular obligation imposed by an order may be

expressed so that it can be waived (on a single or on multiple occasions) if the individual seeks and obtains prior permission for this from a specified person.

25. Subsection (9) defines 'involvement in terrorism-related activity' for the purposes of the Act as:

> a) the commission, preparation or instigation of acts of terrorism;
> b) conduct which facilitates or is intended to facilitate the commission, preparation or instigation of such acts;
> c) conduct which gives encouragement or is intended to give encouragement to the commission, preparation or instigation of such acts;
> d) conduct which gives support or assistance to those known or believed to be involved in terrorism-related activity;

and applies regardless of whether these relate to specific acts or to terrorism in general. By virtue of section 15(1), "terrorism" has the same meaning as in the Terrorism Act 2000 (c. 11).

26. Subsection (10) defines the terms 'derogating obligation' (an obligation incompatible with Article 5 which is of a description set out in a designation order), 'designated derogation' (by reference to the Human Rights Act 1998) and 'designation order'(the order under section 14(1) of the Human Rights Act 1998 by which the derogation is designated).

Section 2: Making of non-derogating control orders

Subsections (1) and (2)

27. Subsection (1) provides that the Secretary of State may make a non-derogating control order if he –

> a) has reasonable grounds for suspecting that the individual is or has been involved in terrorism-related activity; and
> b) considers that it is necessary, for purposes connected with protecting members of the public from a risk of terrorism, to make a control order imposing obligations on the individual.

28. Subsection (2) explains that the Secretary of State can impose a control order on an individual already subject to a control order imposed by the court, only if the court has decided to revoke its control order but has postponed that revocation in order to allow the Secretary of State to decide whether to impose his own.

Subsections (4) and (5)

29.   Subsection (4) states that a non-derogating control order will last for 12 months and may be renewed. Subsection (5) says that a non-derogating control order must state when it will cease to have effect.

Subsections (6) to (8)

30.   Subsection (6) provides that a non-derogating control order may be renewed for 12 months where the Secretary of State considers that it is necessary for the order to continue in force, for purposes connected with protecting members of the public from a risk of terrorism, and that any obligations imposed by the renewed order are necessary for purposes connected with preventing or restricting involvement by the controlled person in terrorism-related activity. Subsection (7) makes further provision about the time from which the 12 month renewal period will begin to run. Subsection (8) states that the instrument renewing a non-derogating order must specify the expiry date of the renewed order.

Subsection (9)

31.   Subsection (9) provides that obligations may be imposed as part of control orders in order to prevent involvement in any terrorism-related activity, not just the activity which gave rise to the grounds for the Secretary of State's suspicion that the controlled person was or had been involved in terrorism-related activity.

Section 3: Supervision by court of making of non-derogating control orders

Subsection (1)

32.   Subsection (1) provides that the Secretary of State can only make a non-derogating control order if:

      a) he has been granted permission to do so by the court;

      b) he has made, and included in the control order, a statement saying that the urgency of the case required him to make the control order without permission from the court; or,

      c) the order is made before 14 March 2005 against an individual who, at the time it is made, is certified under section 21(1) of the Anti-terrorism, Crime and Security Act 2001 (c. 24).

Subsections (2) to (4)

33.   Subsection (2) provides that when the Secretary of State applies to the court for permission to make a non-derogating control order against an individual, the court must decide if the Secretary of State's decision that there are grounds to make the order is obviously flawed. If it determines that the decision is not obviously flawed it will give its permission for the order to be made, and give directions for a full hearing to take place to consider the order as soon as reasonably practicable after it is made. Subsection (3) says that if the Secretary of State makes a control order without permission from the court, he must refer it to the court immediately. Subsection (4) states that the court must begin considering such a reference not later than seven days after the day on which the control order was made.

Subsections (5), (6) and (8)

34.   Subsection (5) provides that the first hearings in connection with non-derogating control orders, in which the court will decide whether to grant permission for the order to be made or will consider the Secretary of State's decision to impose the order without the court's permission, may be ex parte and may take place without the knowledge of the person upon whom the control order will be made. Subsection (6) explains that, in initial hearings on control orders made without the court's permission, the court will consider if the Secretary of State's decision to impose the order was obviously flawed. If it determines that the decision was obviously flawed, the court will quash the order; if it determines that it was not, but that the decision to impose a particular obligation was obviously flawed, it must quash that obligation; in all other cases, it must confirm the order and give directions for a full hearing in relation to the control order to take place. Subsection (8) provides that, in initial hearings on control orders made without the court's permission, the court may quash the certificate which the Secretary of State included in the control order stating that the urgency of the case required that the order be made without first seeking permission from the court.

Subsection (7)

35.   Subsection (7) provides that when the court gives directions for a full hearing in connection with a non-derogating control order to take place, it must make arrangements for the individual in question to be given an opportunity to make representations about the directions already given or the making of further directions,

within seven days of the court's decision.

Subsections (10) and (11)

36.   Subsection (10) explains that in a full hearing on a non-derogating control order, the court will determine whether any of the following decisions of the Secretary of State was flawed:

    a) his decision that he had reasonable grounds for suspecting that the controlled person was or had been involved in terrorism-related activity and his decision that the control order was necessary for purposes connected with protecting members of the public from a risk of terrorism;

    b) his decision to impose each of the obligations in the control order.

37.   Subsection (11) states that in considering the matters coming before it in relation to non-derogating control orders, the court must   apply the principles applicable on an application for judicial review.

Subsections (12) to (14)

38.   Subsections (12) and (13) explain that, in a full hearing on a non-derogating control order, if the court decides that a decision of the Secretary of State was flawed, it may:

    a) quash the control order;

    b) quash one or more of the obligations contained in the control order;

    c) give directions to the Secretary of State for him to revoke or modify the order;

    d) decide that the control order should continue in force.

39.   Subsection (14) provides that the court must discontinue the full hearing on a non-derogating control order if requested to do so by the controlled person.

Section 4: Power of the court to make derogating control orders

Subsections (1) to (4)

40.   Subsection (1) provides for the court to hold an immediate preliminary hearing on an application from the Secretary of State to decide whether to make a derogating

control order against an individual. If it determines to make such an order, it is required to give directions for a full hearing to take place to determine whether to confirm the order, with or without modifications.

41.   Subsection (2) states that the preliminary hearing may be ex parte and may take place without the knowledge of the person upon whom the control order will be made.

42.   Subsection (3) sets out the tests which the court must consider when deciding if a derogating control order can be made. It must appear to the court that:

    a) there is material which (if not disproved) is capable of being relied on by the court as establishing that the individual is or has been involved in terrorism-related activity.

    b) there are reasonable grounds for believing that the obligations in the control order are necessary for purposes connected with protecting members of the public from a risk of terrorism.

    c) the risk in question arises out of or is associated with a public emergency in respect of which there is a designated derogation from all or part of Article 5 of the ECHR.

    d) that the obligations in the control order are of a description set out in the designation order.

43.   Subsection (4) provides that the obligations the court may impose between the time when the order is made and the time when the court makes its determination at the full hearing include any obligations which it has reasonable grounds for believing to be necessary for purposes connected with preventing or restricting involvement by the controlled person in terrorism-related activity.

Subsection (5) to (7)

44.   Subsection (5) provides that, at a full hearing on a derogating control order, the court may confirm or revoke the control order. If it revokes the order, it may direct that the order be treated as having been quashed under the terms of this Act. Subsection (6) states that, when confirming a derogating control order, the court may modify the obligations imposed by the order and direct that the obligation be treated as having been quashed under the terms of this Act.

45.   Subsection (7) explains the tests which the court must apply when considering whether to confirm a derogating control order at a full hearing. It can only confirm the

order if:

a) it is satisfied on the balance of probabilities that the person is or has been involved in terrorism-related activities;
b) it considers that the imposition of a control order is necessary for purposes connected with protecting members of the public from a risk of terrorism;
c) it appears to the court that the risk arises out of or is associated with a public emergency in respect of which there is a designated derogation from all or part of Article 5; and
d) the obligation(s) are of a description set out in the designation order.

Subsections (8) to (13)

46. Subsection (8) provides that a derogating control order will last six months, unless it ceases to have effect either because it is revoked or because it would otherwise continue beyond the period provided for in section 6 (ie there has been no order within the relevant period confirming that it continues to be necessary for the Secretary of State to have the power to impose derogating obligations) It can also continue for more than six months if the court renews it. The renewal procedure is described in subsection (9).

47. As subsection (10) explains, when the court is considering whether to renew a derogating control order on an application from the Secretary of State, it may only do so if:

a) the court considers that it is necessary for the derogating control order to continue in force for purposes connected with protecting members of the public from a risk of terrorism;
b) it appears to the court that the risk arises out of or is associated with a public emergency in respect of which there is a designated derogation from all or part of Article 5 ECHR;
c) the obligations are of a description that continues to be set out in a designation order; and,
d) the court considers that the obligations imposed in the renewed order are necessary for purposes connected with preventing or restricting the controlled person's involvement in terrorism-related activity.

48. Subsection (11) provides that the court may extend a control order in order to allow it to continue to operate while proceedings on an application for renewal take place. Subection (12) notes that if a control order is extended under subsection (11) the renewed control order will be valid for six months from the date at which the order

would have ceased to have effect.

49.   Subsection (13) states that obligations may be imposed as part of a control order in order to prevent involvement in any terrorism-related activity, not just the activity which led the court to conclude that the individual was or had been involved in terrorism-related activity.

Section 5: Arrest and detention pending derogating control order

Subsections (1) to (6)

50.   Subsections (1) to (4) provide for the arrest and detention of an individual in respect of whom the Secretary of State is seeking a derogating control order. He may be arrested and detained for 48 hours in the first instance, with the possibility of the court extending the detention for a further 48 hours. A constable may arrest someone under this section if the Secretary of State has applied to the court for a derogating control order to be made and the constable considers that the individual's arrest and detention are necessary to ensure the individual is able to receive notice of the order when it is made. The constable must take the arrested individual to an appropriate "designated place" (as defined in Paragraph 1(1) of Schedule 8 to the Terrorism Act 2000). If it considers it necessary to ensure that the individual is available to receive any notice, the court may during the first 48 hours of such detention, extend the period of detention for up to a further 48 hours.   Subsection (5) provides that the power of detention shall cease once a person becomes bound by a derogating control order (ie once it has been served) or once the court dismisses the application from the Secretary of State. Subsection (6) provides that an individual who has the powers of a constable in one part of the UK can exercise the power of arrest under this section in any part of the UK.

Subsections (7), (8) and (10)

51.   Subsection (7) provides that an individual detained under section 5 will be deemed to be in 'police detention' under the Police and Criminal Evidence Act 1984 (c. 60) for England and Wales, and the Police and Criminal Evidence (Northern Ireland) Order 1989 (N. I. 12) for Northern Ireland. Subsection (8) applies certain provisions of Schedule 8 to the Terrorism Act 2000 (c. 11) to the individual with appropriate adjustments. Subsection (10) states that a 'designated place' is a place designated under paragraph 1(1) of Schedule 8 to the Terrorism Act 2000.

Subsection (9)

52.   Subsection (9) states that detention under this section may be incompatible with the right to liberty under Article 5 ECHR if there is a designated derogation in connection with these powers, and the derogation in connection with these powers arises from the same public emergency as the derogation in connection with derogating control orders.

Section 6: Duration of derogating control orders

Subsection (1)

53.   Subsection (1) provides that a derogating control order has effect at a time only if the relevant derogation is still in force and that time is not more than 12 months after the making of the order designating the derogation, or after the making of an order by the Secretary of State declaring that it continues to be necessary for him to have the power to impose derogating obligations under that derogation.

Subsections (2) to (7)

54.   Subsections (2) to (7) set out the procedure for the Secretary of State to make order of the kind referred to in subsection (1) (ie declaring that it continues to be necessary for him to have the power to impose derogating obligations).

Section 7: Modification, notification and proof of orders etc.

Subsection (1)

55.   Subsection (1) provides that a controlled person can apply to the Secretary of State for the revocation or modification of a non-derogating control order if there has been a change of circumstances affecting the order, and the Secretary of State shall have a duty to consider the application.

Subsections (2) and (3)

56.   Subsection (2) allows the Secretary of State, at any time during the operation of a non-derogating control order, to revoke the order, or to relax or remove an obligation imposed by the order. The Secretary of State may make any modifications

to the obligations imposed by the order that he considers necessary for purposes connected with preventing or restricting involvement by the controlled person in terrorism-related activity. Subsection (2) also allows for the modification of a non-derogating control order by mutual consent. Subsection (3) provides that the Secretary of State may not, however, make any modifications which turn a non-derogating control order into one which imposes a derogating obligation.

Subsections (3) to (7)

57.   Subsection (4) allows the Secretary of State and the controlled person to apply to the court for the revocation or modification of a derogating control order. Subsection (5) states that the court can modify obligations imposed by the derogating control order if the effect of the modification is to remove or relax an obligation, the modification is by mutual consent or the court considers the modification to be necessary for purposes connected with preventing or restricting the controlled person's involvement in terrorism-related activity. Subsection (6) says that modification of a derogating control order cannot involve imposing derogating obligations unless the court considers the modification to be necessary for purposes connected with protecting members of the public from a risk of terrorism, and it appears to the court that the risk arises out of, or is associated with, the public emergency in respect of which there is a designated derogation.

58.   Subsection (7) requires the court, if it considers that derogating obligations no longer need to be imposed as part of a derogating control order, to revoke the control order in its entirety.

Subsections (8) to (11)

59.   Subsection (8) requires notice of the imposition, renewal or modification of a control order (other than a relaxation or modification with consent) to be given to the controlled person in person if the imposition, renewal or modification is to have effect. Subsection (9) states that a constable or other person authorised by the Secretary of State may enter any premises where he has reasonable grounds to believe the subject of a control order to be, and to search those premises, in order to serve notice upon the individual. Subsection (10) requires the Secretary of State, if he revokes or modifies a control order under subsection (2)(b) or (c), to give notice to the controlled person of the revocation or modification and of the date from which the revocation or modification is effective. Subsection (11) explains how a control order,

or the renewal, revocation or modification of an order, may be proved.

Section 8: Criminal investigations after making of control order

Subsections (1) to (6)

60.   Subsection (1) provides that this section applies where it appears to the Secretary of State that an individual's suspected involvement in terrorism-related activity may have involved the commission of an offence relating to terrorism, and that the commission of that offence is being or would fall to be investigated by a police force. Subsection (2) requires the Secretary of State to consult the chief police officer of that police force about the evidence relating to the individual before he makes a control order to see if there is evidence available that could realistically be used for the purposes of a prosecution of the individual for an offence relating to terrorism. Subsection (3) requires the Secretary of State to inform that chief police officer when he has made a control order. Subsection (4) requires the chief police officer to keep the investigation of the individual's conduct under review for the duration of the control order to see if prosecution for a terrorism-related offence becomes possible.

61.   Subsection (5) requires the chief police officer to consult the relevant prosecuting authority about the carrying out of his functions under the section, but only, when the control order has been made, to the extent that he considers it appropriate in the light of his review of the investigation into the individual's conduct. Subsection (6) provides that the chief police officer's duty to consult the relevant prosecuting authority may have been satisfied by consultation that took place wholly or partly before this Act was passed.

Subsections (7) to (9)

62.   Subsection (7) defines 'chief officer', 'police force' and 'relevant prosecuting authority'. Subsection (8) contains transitional provisions in relation to the Serious Organised Crime Agency (necessary since at the time of the passage of the Prevention of Terrorism Act, the Bill establishing the Serious Organised Crime Agency, which is intended to subsume the National Crime Squad, was still before Parliament). Subsection (9) clarifies references to 'the Scottish Drug Enforcement Agency' and 'the Director' of that agency in subsection (7).

Section 9: Offences

Subsections (1) to (3)

63.   Subsection (1) provides that an individual is guilty of an offence if he breaches, without reasonable excuse, an obligation imposed on him by a control order. Subsection (2) creates an offence in connection with a failure, without reasonable excuse, to report to a specified person when first returning to the UK as required by the terms of a control order, when the order has ceased to have effect. Subsection (3) provides that any individual is guilty of an offence if he intentionally obstructs a person delivering a notice setting out the terms of the control order in accordance with section 7(9).

Subsections (4) to (10)

64.   Subsection (4) provides that a person who is guilty of an offence under section 9(1) or 9(2) will be liable on conviction on indictment to a prison sentence of up to 5 years or a fine and (in England and Wales) on summary conviction to a prison sentence of up to 12 months or a fine. On summary conviction in Scotland and Northern Ireland a person is liable to a prison sentence of up to 6 months or a fine. Subsection (5) contains transitional provisions in relation to subsection (4) since pending the bringing into force of Section 154(1) of the Criminal Justice Act 2003 the maximum available sentence is 6 months.

65.   Subsection (6) provides that where an individual is convicted of an offence under section 9(1) or (2) it is not to be open to the court in England and Wales to make a conditional discharge order. It also makes similar provisions for the other jurisdictions.

66.   Subsection (7) provides that a person who is guilty of an offence under section 9(3) shall be liable upon summary conviction, in England and Wales, to a prison sentence of up to 51 weeks or a fine. In Scotland and Northern Ireland summary conviction will lead to a prison sentence of up to 6 months or a fine. Subsection (8)

contains transitional provisions relating to subsection (7) since pending the bringing into force of section 281(5) of the Criminal Justice Act 2003, the maximum available sentence is 6 months.

67.   Subsections (9) and (10) provide that the new offence of obstructing the service of a control order is an arrestable offence (not requiring a warrant).

Section 10: Appeals relating to non-derogating control orders

Subsections (1) to (3)

68.   Subsection (1) provides that the controlled person may appeal against the renewal or non-consensual modification of a non-derogating control order. When a control order is renewed with modifications, subsection (2) makes it clear that the individual concerned may appeal against any or all of the modifications. Subsection (3) provides that if a person applies to the Secretary of State for the modification or revocation of a non-derogating control order, he may appeal against any decision by the Secretary of State on the application.

Subsections (4) to (6)

69.   Subsection (4) provides that when the court hears an appeal against the renewal of a non-derogating control order or against a decision not to revoke a non-derogating control order, it must determine whether either or both of the following decisions of the Secretary of State was flawed:

> a) his decision that it was necessary to renew or continue the control order for purposes connected with protecting members of the public from a risk of terrorism; and
> b) his decision that it was necessary to renew or continue each of the particular obligations in the control order in question for purposes connected with preventing or restricting involvement by the controlled person in terrorism-related activity.

70.   Subsection (5) provides that when the court hears an appeal against the

modification of a non-derogating control order (whether on renewal or otherwise), it must determine whether or not the Secretary of State's decision that the modification was necessary for purposes connected with preventing or restricting involvement by the controlled person in terrorism-related activity was flawed. When the court hears an appeal against a decision not to modify a non-derogating control order, it must determine whether or not the Secretary of State's decision that the obligation was still necessary for purposes connected with preventing or restricting involvement by the controlled person in terrorism-related activity was flawed.

71.   Subsection (6) provides that the court must apply the principles applicable on an application for judicial review when determining matters mentioned in subsections (4) and (5).

Subsections (7) and (8)

72.   Subsection (7) provides that if a court upholds an appeal against a decision of the Secretary of State in an appeal under this section, it can:

    a) quash the control order;
    b) quash one or more of the particular obligations in the control order;
    c) give directions to the Secretary of State to revoke the control order or modify the obligations it imposes.

73.   Subsection (8) states that in every other case, the court must dismiss the appeal.

Section 11: Jurisdiction and appeals in relation to control order decisions etc.

Subsections (1) to (3)

74.   Subsection (1) provides that control order decisions and derogation matters are not to be questioned in any legal proceedings other than proceedings in the court or on appeal from such proceedings. The court is defined in section 15(1) to mean the High Court or Court of Session as appropriate. By virtue of subsection (2) the relevant court will be able to consider matters alleged by the appellant to raise Human Rights issues in respect of control order procedures. Subsection (3) says that appeals from any determination of the court in control order proceedings can only be on a question of

law.

Subsection (4)

75.   Subsection (4) states that only the Secretary of State can appeal against the judgment of the court on an application under section 3(1)(a) (when it gives permission for him to impose a non-derogating control order) or on a reference under sction 3(3)(a) (when it confirms a non-derogating control order made without its permission). (This is because the controlled person is able to challenge the decision in the full hearing that automatically takes place following directions by the court under section 3(2)(c) or 3(6)(b) or (c))

Subsections (5) to (8)

76.   Subsection (5) gives effect to the Schedule (which sets out further provision in relation to control order proceedings and relevant appeal proceedings). Subsections (6), (7) and (8) define the terms 'control order proceedings', 'control order decision' and 'derogation matter' respectively.

Section 12: Effect of court's decisions on convictions

Subsections (1) to (3)

77.   Subsections (1) and (2) provide that a person convicted of an offence under section 9(1) or (2) may appeal against their conviction if the control order or obligation which they breached is subsequently quashed in control order proceedings (or on appeal from such proceedings). Subsection (3) provides that when an appeal is brought under this section, the relevant court must allow the appeal and quash the conviction. These provisions need to be read in association with paragraph 8 of the Schedule.

Subsections (4) to (7)

78.   Subsections (4) to (7) make it clear that an appeal may be brought notwithstanding the fact that an earlier appeal may already have been brought and set out other matters in relation to such an appeal.

Subsection (8)

79.   Subsection (8) amends section 133 of the Criminal Justice Act 1988 (c. 33) (compensation for miscarriages of justice) to permit compensation to be awarded on an application under that section. This would allow an individual to claim compensation if, for example, he had been convicted for breaching the conditions of an order and subject to a penalty, and where the relevant Control Order in question was subsequently quashed by a court.

Section 13: Duration of sections 1 to 9

Subsections (1) to (3)

80.   Subsection (1) provides that sections 1 to 9 of this Act expire 12 months after the day on which this Act was passed (11 March 2005) but under subsection (2), they may be renewed for a period not exceeding one year by order made by statutory instrument. (Subsection (2) also includes provision for repeal and revival of sections 1 to 9). Subsection (3) states that, before making such an order, the Secretary of State must consult the independent reviewer appointed under section 14, the Intelligence Services Commissioner and the Director-General of the Security Service.

Subsections (4) to (7)

81.   Subsections (4) to (7) deal with the procedure for making an order under this section. Subsection (4) provides that a draft of any order under this section must be approved by both Houses of Parliament before the order can be made. However, subsections (5) and (6) allow the Secretary of State to make an order under this section without the prior approval of Parliament if the order contains a declaration that the order had to be made without prior approval because of the urgency involved in the situation. In such cases, the Secretary of State must refer the order to Parliament after making it. If Parliament does not then approve the order within 40 days, it will cease to have effect at the end of that period. However, as subsection (7) makes clear, if such an order does lapse after 40 days, this will not affect anything done previously on the basis of the order, nor will it prevent the Secretary of State making a new order to the same or similar effect as the one which has ceased to have effect.

Subsections (8) to (9)

82.   Subsection (8) states that the expiration or repeal of sections 1 to 9 does not prevent or affect:

> a) the court's consideration of a reference under section 3(3)(a) (to review a decision by the Secretary of State to impose a control order without the court's permission);
> b) the court's consideration of a hearing under section 3(2)(c), section 3(6)(b) or section 3(6)(c) (full hearings to review the making of a non-derogating control order);
> c) the court's consideration of a hearing to confirm the making of a derogating control order;
> d) the bringing or continuation of any appeal or further appeal relating to the proceedings mentioned in paragraphs (a) to (c).

83.   But proceedings may only be brought or continued by virtue of subsection (8) so far as they are for the purposes of determining if a certificate of the Secretary of State, a control order or an obligation imposed by such an order are to be quashed or treated as quashed.

84.   Subsection (9) confirms that the Act does not permit a control order to be effective when the provision under which it was made has expired or been repealed.

Section 14: Reporting and review

Subsection (1)

85.   Subsection (1) provides that the Secretary of State must report to Parliament on a 3 monthly basis on the exercise of his control order powers during that period. A copy of each report must be laid before Parliament.

Subsections (2) to (6)

86.   Subsection (2) states that the Secretary of State must appoint a person to review the operation of the Act. Under subsection (3), this reviewer must review the

operation of the Act nine months after it came into effect, and every twelve months thereafter. Subsections (4) and (6) provide that the reviewer must send his report to the Secretary of State as soon as reasonably practicable after carrying out the review, and that the Secretary of State must lay a copy of the review before Parliament. Subsection (5) states that the reviewer must include in his report his opinions on:

> a) the implications for the operation of the Act of any amendments to the law relating to terrorism which the Secretary of State has proposed; and
> b) the extent (if any) to which the Secretary of State has used his power to make non-derogating control orders in urgent cases without the permission of the court.

Subsection (8)

87.   Subsection (8) defines the terms 'control order powers' and 'relevant 3 month period' for the purposes of this section.

Section 15: General interpretation

Subsection (1)

88.   Subsection (1) sets out definitions of a number of terms contained in the Act.

Subsections (3) and (4)

89.   Subsection (3) states that the Secretary of State or the court has the power to state when any revocation or modification of a control order which he or it has decided to make will take effect. It also confirms that the court can postpone the effect of any revocation of a derogating control order either pending an appeal or to allow the Secretary of State time to consider whether to make a non-derogating control order against the same person. Subsection (4) provides that a failure of the Secretary of State to consider an application for a revocation or modification of the order by an individual shall be treated as a decision not to modify or revoke the order.

Section 16: Other supplemental provisions

Subsections (2) and (3)

90.   Subsection (2) provides for repeals, including the repeal of certain sections in Part 4 of the Anti-terrorism, Crime and Security Act 2001 (c. 24) (ATCSA). Under subsection (3), subsection (2) came into force on 14 March 2005.

Subsection (4)

91.   Subsection (4) provides a transitional saving in relation to appeals under section 25 ATCSA. It enables outstanding appeals under section 25 ATCSA to be completed. It also enables outstanding appeals further to any decisions by the Special Immigration Appeals Commission (SIAC) on appeals under section 25 ATCSA to be completed. Any proceedings that result from appeals against determinations by SIAC under section 25 ATCSA can likewise be completed. However, no other proceedings before SIAC under Part 4 ATCSA can be commenced or continued after the time at which sections 21 to 32 ATCSA are repealed.

Schedule

92.   The Schedule makes provision relating to and for the purposes of control order proceedings in the High Court and Court of Session and proceedings on appeal from such proceedings.

Paragraph 1

93.   This paragraph provides a definition of 'relevant powers' and 'relevant appeal proceedings'.

94.   The relevant powers are the existing powers to make rules of court for the High Court, the Court of Appeal and the Court of Session, so far as those powers are exercisable in relation to control order proceedings and relevant appeal proceedings.

Paragraph 2

95.   This paragraph imposes a general duty on persons exercising the relevant powers to have regard to (a) the need to secure that control orders are properly reviewed and (b) the need to secure that disclosures of information are not made where they would be contrary to the public interest.

Paragraph 3

96.   This paragraph makes special provision for the initial exercise of the relevant powers in relation to England and Wales and Northern Ireland. The Lord Chancellor may exercise those relevant powers to make rules for control order proceedings and relevant appeal proceedings on the first occasion that those powers are exercised after the passing of the Act (instead of the Civil Procedure Rule Committee and the Northern Ireland Supreme Court Rules Committee).

97.   Sub-paragraph (3) provides that the Lord Chancellor must consult the Lord Chief Justice of England and Wales and the Lord Chief Justice of Northern Ireland, before making any rules in relation to those jurisdictions.

98.   Sub-paragraph (5) provides that the rules of court made by the Lord Chancellor must be laid before Parliament and if not approved by a resolution of each House within 40 days of their making, they cease to have effect.

99.   Sub-paragraph (6) provides that if the rules cease to have effect in accordance with sub-paragraph (5), (a) that does not affect anything previously done in reliance on those rules; (b) the Lord Chancellor has the power to make new rules; and (c) the new rules may include rules to the same or similar effect as the rules that have ceased to have effect.

Paragraph 4

100.   This paragraph makes further provision for rules of court made in exercise of the relevant powers.

101.   Sub-paragraphs (1) and (2) set out the matters for which such rules may make provision. Rules may provide, for example, that proceedings are to be conducted in the absence of the controlled person, and his legal representative, when the court hears sensitive evidence in closed session. Rules may also allow the court to give the controlled person a summary of the evidence taken in his absence.

102.   Sub-paragraph (3) sets out the procedures that must be secured by such rules.

Rules must make provision:

- To require the Secretary of State (subject to rules made under sub-paragraph (3)(b) to (g)) to disclose all 'relevant material', which is defined in sub-paragraph (5) as any information or other material that is available to the Secretary of State and relevant to the matters in the proceedings and the reasons for decisions to which the proceedings relate.

- To allow the Secretary of State an opportunity to apply to the court for permission not to disclose relevant material to anyone other than the court or persons appointed under paragraph 7 of the Schedule (the special advocates).

- To ensure that the court always considers such an application in the absence of the controlled person (or any other relevant party) and his legal representative.

- To ensure that the court must give permission for material to be withheld where the court considers that disclosure of that material would be contrary to the public interest.

- To ensure that where the court grants permission for material not to be disclosed the court considers requiring the Secretary of State to provide the relevant party and his legal representative with a summary of the material.

- To ensure that, where the Secretary of State elects not to disclose relevant material, or provide a summary, the court may prevent the Secretary of State from relying on that material, or matters required to be summarised. The court may also require the Secretary of State to withdraw any allegation or argument to which that material (or matters required to be summarised) relates.

Paragraph 5

103.   This paragraph provides that the rules may also allow the controlled person, or the Secretary of State, to apply for an order requiring the anonymity of the controlled person, even before court proceedings have begun.

Paragraph 6

104.   This paragraph provides for the court to call on advisers, appointed for the purpose by the Lord Chancellor, and to hear and dispose of proceedings with the

assistance of those advisers.

Paragraph 7

105.   This paragraph makes provision for the appointment of qualified lawyers (to be known as "special advocates") to represent the interests of a relevant party to control order proceedings and relevant appeal proceedings where that party and his legal representative are excluded from the proceedings. The special advocate is not responsible to the party whom he represents.

Paragraph 8

106.   This paragraph provides that, for the purposes of section 9(1) and 9(2), where a court quashes a control order or an obligation imposed by it (or where it revokes a control order or obligation and directs that the Act shall have effect as if the order or obligation had been quashed), that order or obligation shall be treated as though it had never been made or imposed. But the quashing of a control order or obligation does not prevent the Secretary of State from exercising his power to make a new order to the same or similar effect or from relying on the same matters in doing so.

Paragraph 9

107.   This paragraph amends section 18 of the Regulation of Investigatory Powers Act 2000 (c. 23) to allow for the admission of interception evidence in control order proceedings or any proceedings arising from such proceedings.

Paragraph 10

108.   This paragraph amends paragraph 2 of Schedule 1 to the Supreme Court Act 1981 (c. 54) to allocate control order proceedings to the Queen's Bench Division of the High Court.

COMMENCEMENT

109.   The Act came into force on Royal Assent, except section 13(2) which came into force on 14 March 2005.

HANSARD REFERENCES

The following table sets out the dates and Hansard references for each stage of this Act's passage through Parliament.

Stage	Date	Hansard reference
House of Commons		
Introduction	22 February 2005	Vol 431 Cols 152 – 170
Second Reading	23 February 2005	Vol 431 Cols 333 – 448
Committee	28 February 2005	Vol 431 Cols 663 – 768
Report and Third Reading	28 February 2005	Vol 431 Cols 768 – 788
House of Lords		
Introduction	1 March 2005	Vol 670 Col 114
Second Reading	1 March 2005	Vol 670 Cols 116 – 219
Committee	3 March 2005	Vol 670 Cols 359 – 383
	7 March 2005	Vol 670 Cols 482 – 556
Report	8 March 2005	Vol 670 Cols 627 – 704

Third Reading	8 March 2005	Vol 670 Cols 724 – 726
Commons Consideration of Lords Amendments	9 March 2005	Vol 431 Cols 1573 – 1657
Lords Consideration of Commons Reasons and Amendments	10 March 2005	Vol 670 Cols 845 – 919
Commons Consideration of Lords Reasons and Amendments	10 March 2005	Vol 431 Cols 1761 – 1795
Lords Consideration of Commons Reasons and Amendments	10 March 2005	Vol 670 Cols 999 – 1018
Commons Consideration of Lords Reasons and Amendments	10 March 2005	Vol 431 Cols 1796 – 1826
Lords Consideration of Commons Reasons and Amendments	10 March 2005	Vol 670 Col 1019 – 1032
Commons Consideration of Lords Reasons and Amendments	10 March 2005	Vol 431 Cols 1826 – 1853
Lords Consideration of Commons Reasons and Amendments	10 March 2005	Vol 670 Col 1032 – 1057
Commons Consideration of Lords Reasons and Amendments	10 March 2005	Vol 431 Cols 1854 - 1879
Lords Consideration of Commons Reasons and Amendments	10 March 2005	Vol 670 Col 1057 – 1066
Royal Assent House of Commons House of Lords	 11 March 2005 11 March 2005	 Vol 431 Col 1880 Vol 670 Col 1066

© Crown copyright 2005

Printed in the UK by The Stationery Office Limited
under the authority and superintendence of Carol Tullo, Controller of
Her Majesty's Stationery Office and Queen's Printer of Acts of Parliament.

4/2005   304858   19585

Published by TSO (The Stationery Office) and available from:

Online
www.tso.co.uk/bookshop

Mail, Telephone, Fax & E-mail
TSO
PO Box 29, Norwich NR3 1GN
Telephone orders/General enquiries 0870 600 5522
Fax orders 0870 600 5533
Order through the Parliamentary Hotline *Lo-call* 0845 7 023474
Email book.orders@tso.co.uk
Textphone 0870 240 3701

TSO Shops
123 Kingsway, London WC2B 6PQ
020 7242 6393 Fax 020 7242 6394
68–69 Bull Street, Birmingham B4 6AD
0121 236 9696 Fax 0121 236 9699
9–21 Princess Street, Manchester M60 8AS
0161 834 7201 Fax 0161 833 0634
16 Arthur Street, Belfast BT1 4GD
028 9023 8451 Fax 028 9023 5401
18–19 High Street, Cardiff CF10 1PT
029 2039 5548 Fax 029 2038 4347
71 Lothian Road, Edinburgh EH3 9AZ
0870 606 5566 Fax 0870 606 5588

The Parliamentary Bookshop
12 Bridge Street, Parliament Square,
London SW1A 2JX
Telephone orders/General enquiries 020 7219 3890
Fax orders 020 7219 3866

Accredited Agents
(see Yellow Pages)

and through good booksellers

ISBN 0-10-560205-1

9 780105 602057